Garrulous Waters:
An intimate autobiographical poetic

By

Allison A. Baker

1stBooks - rev. 04/27/07

Also, there will be signs in sun and moon and stars and on the earth anguish of nations, not knowing the way out because of the roaring of the sea and it's agitation
—Luke 21:25

These are rocks hidden below water in your love feasts while they feast with you, shepherds that feed themselves without fear; waterless clouds carried this way and that by winds; trees in late autumn (but) fruitless having died twice, having been uprooted, wild waves of the sea that foam up their own causes for shame, stars with no set course, for which the blackness of darkness stands reserved forever.
—Jude: 12,13

And the sea gave up those dead in it...
—Revelations 20: 13.

This book is dedicated to:

Chelsea, Gabrielle and Nina

GRATITUDE/ACKNOWLEDGEMENT

In my short life there have been so many people that I needed, so many teachers, therapists, nurturers, sisters, brothers, family, friends...it would be typical of my misfortune to list everyone and forget that one special person. I will not tempt fate by naming names but know this that while words can transform, up-build and heal, but they cannot convey the depth of my gratitude to the family and friends who have taken time to journey with me and to love me. I don't have to tell you who you are. I can't tell you what you already know but for the record...simply put...Thank you

Agape—Namaste

TABLE OF CONTENTS

FOREWARD xi

THE RISING LEVEL 1

Untitled 3
Pamela 4
Suzy Q 6
Daddy 7
Venita 10
Definitions 12
Cinnamon Janet 13
No Escape 14
"Excuse Me Nurse, Where Is My Baby" 15
Earth To Seed 16
Family Tree 17
Drum The Skins 18

RAIN FALLS INTO THE OCEAN ON ANY GIVEN DAY 19

Puzzle 21
Obsess 23
Roses 25
He 26
One More Dance 28
Nobody's Fool 29
Of Mice And Men 30
Sugar Daddy 31
Gunfire 32
Kiss 33
To My One Night Man 34
Untitled 35
Ocean Pull 36
Lushness 37
Compromise 38

THE FLOOD 39

Flood 41
Poetry 42
Garrulous 43
Sesame Street 45
Opium Song 46
Cardboard Home 47
Life Without The ID 49

FROM A PUDDLE TO A STREAM UNTIL THE OCEAN 51

In The Mirror 53
She's On Time 55

FOREWARD

There is no escaping the fact that, there are two most powerful moments in your life-your first breath and your first decision. The first moment is one that is controlled entirely by fate and the instinct to survive. The second moment is a powerful impetus that changes the size and scope of your existence. Our choices are what transform dreams into reality. When the time comes to cash in those dreams, you hold your breath and jump feet first into the vast unknown. This collection of poetry and this book represents my venture into the unfamiliar. I am someone who thinks too much and runs away from reality, but poetry has always buoyed me. If truth be told, I began this path of poetic expression from early as I can remember. As a child, I would memorize rap song lyrics, so that I could recite them at school the next day. In Junior High School, I would write my own "rhymes" which were essentially, poems. This penning of verse continued for many years until my writing, as in all artistic craft, reached a point where it cultivated a pearl. Officially cultured, the collection in this book began in 1996. My writing prior to this was speculative and passive, unripe. The reason for this outside of my obvious lack of experience was that I was not able to tap into my emotional resources to arouse the poignancy that I needed to express. Everything that I wrote before I made my decision to become a young mother was a backburner effort. My growth as a single mother (young at age 19) and all of the self-reflection that accompanies this role aided me in understanding the difficult layers of my life.

My mother died when I was 17 and her death emphasized so many of my decisions. Shadowing me in the men that I chose, the depth of my alcoholism, my depression and ultimately my baby lust that saved me from suicide. However, the revolution of motherhood was only the beginning.

In the year of 1996, while planning to go to a family reunion in Florida, my eldest sister Pamela and her husband Norman were killed in a car accident. They were driving to her husband's family reunion in New Orleans; the accident took place in Washington, D.C. Riding in the backseat of the car were their 3 children whose ages were 8, 5, and 1 years old. It is not easy to convey this tragedy, yet this was not the only calamity to occur that year. In December 1996, my sister Susan was murdered by her drug addicted boyfriend. She disappeared while cooking dinner for a Christmas Eve celebration. We filed a missing persons report and the police found her body the day after Christmas. Susan is survived by two children (my niece and nephew).

Earlier, I mentioned two powerful moments, but what is most remarkable of the two instances is when we are forced to watch those that we love, either take their first breath (or last) or transform their life with a choice. The powerlessness of this vantage point adds a spectator position to our interactions with one another especially when it is a shared trauma. It is this watching, observing, examining and introspection that reaches a point where we must appease our conscious with various forms of spirituality. By tapping into positivism, growth and love, you are guaranteed spiritual nourishment and definite survival. I try to be the spirit that I want to see in this world because as a survivor, I know that survivors will never know an empty struggle. My father and my family know this as we move forward in our respective futures. I think this is what anchors us to the mundane and grounds us in hope.

Having endured so much personal tragedy, I chose poetry as the vehicle to orchestrate the maelstrom of my emotions. The word garrulous means rambling or talking excessively which is the state of mind that is most conducive to healing. My poetic ramblings are garrulous and like water. When I think of water, it has always been used as a symbol for human emotions as represented in Theology, mythology, and astrology. When emotions run fluidly through your mind, you are experiencing garrulous waters. The resulting verbal and cerebral expressions of this flood are laced into the layers of my prose to convey the intricacies of my melancholy. Sentiments, feelings, are salient yet watery. It is like my heart is filled with Garrulous water. Word filled waters, rising and full of waves. What happens when your tears begin to sound like a song? A piece of personal music whose chords hum and vibrate with your voice and your moaning. This is my autobiographical poetic, the scheme of my fate. It is this poignancy that compels me to share my perspective in the only tongue that I've ever known, the tongue of a poet.

So, while I occupy only flesh, blood and bone, I am carrying an ocean of experience. I feel destiny pulling me closer to you, my listeners, and therapists. I am approaching you, not out of egotism; it is because of my human desire to survive. I am writing to actualize...because, if I want to stay afloat, I've got to lose some baggage.

THE RISING LEVEL

I can't take anymore
Bad news!
I can't
I won't
Hear anything else!
I can't

Today
I am going to finally escape
The news that my mother really is dead
In my dreams she is not
Because breast cancer does not really
exist

My sister does not think that she is the
Christ in her schizophrenic frenzy calling
me at 2 a.m. to say
That there are moonbeams in her eyes
that will make her a movie star
And a pop sensation but
She can't sing or carry one note anywhere
But she strokes the keyboard
She bought it with begging money
It is cradled close she calls it by the names
of the lost babies
Four born still
Born dead
She sings songs to our daddy
My father is not an alcoholic
Drowning out his sorrows
Moaning lost pieces of his lost soul

"It is unnatural for a parent to outlive
their children"

The daughters
Were killed
One in an accident
One was shot to death

NO!
No, no, no
No more news
Of death cruelty insanity
This world is the devils
Playpen

We are earthly pawn
I can't take anymore bad news!
Family ties cannot bind me
But these scars run so deep
They are the bloodlines
They are the definition
Of my life

Is it family perdition?

I am running from the flames
From the kindred kindling
Until I
Finally
Escape into my own face
& Search thru my soul of resilience
To see my empty acceptance
Fate forcefully pulls my hand along the
journey

I am accompanied by my family
They make me want to be distracted
To cope

Until one day
We have peace
A piece of me weeps
A piece of me laughs
A piece of me hides
From the devolvement
A piece of me hides

Allison A. Baker

PAMELA

Allow my anthem
Please consider
Her skin was
Like toasted almonds

Her eyes
Dimmed the sunset

But
She wore wisdom
On her sleeve

She was one daughter

One mother

My sister

The eldest

Held my hand with zeal
From childhood
To adolescence

Thru early lessons
Of single mother
Reality checks
That bounced
Back and forth
Until one day she was gone

For now...
I now wear the brand
Of sorrow
That I advertise
As a baby sister
Who survived
Her elder
At an early age

And she had no rhythm
And she was a stoic
And she told me often
Of how selfish I was in my prime
with personal excuses
And she pervaded me

And often she drove over 20 miles
To bring me groceries
And listened to struggled poems
And stayed up a sundry of nights
With worries
Creasing sheets
Regarding me
Baby sister

Who now lives
To inhale
Exhale
Life, like
One who is possessed
To possess my life
Although less one life

Hers

Who am I to breathe?

To open my eyes and see the day
And spend the day
With my children
And her children
Who carry the mark
Of foundlings
Of loss

It's in their eyes

Somehow
It's all in their eyes
That something that expressions
Written
Or
Artwork
Could never portray
The day she died
And he by her side

Norman

Her love
And she

Laughing into an echo
Of memories shared
Eternal amen's

Of the unknown
Yet my sister's sprouts
Have not grown
Someday
The youngest baby
Will recognize
Her mama's laugh
Off in the distance of faint
memory

Allison A. Baker

SUZY Q

Dark, Moist, Sweet
Crème filling
In the sandwich cake called Suzy Q's

These favored by me at age 3
My sister Susan brought me a cake
everyday, I remember Susan

& they say that night is a female
My sister was shot by a male at night

She was dark
Sweet
Chocolate beauty
Cocoa Rich - Love

My father identified her through her
dental records

There was no rainbow for the flood of
tears.
No appointed warmth to rounded,
slumped shoulders
Children motherless now vomit tragedy

Little girl blue
Little boy blue

Niece and Nephew always remember
your mother's love

Like a memory carrying a piece of
chocolate cake
Partake of the sweet invocation
&
Occupy the recollection of her wide gap
tooth smile and her unconditional
edifying
Remember her while the sweet texture
rolls on your tongue
remember Suzy Q

She would come to your aid before you
could hang up the phone,
She was there by my side
But she loved a fool
He loved her to death

Moans, sighs, rocking, grasping,
grasping, grasping, tears

Susan, I will not remember you as muddy
water
Nor oily, polluted and bloody soil

I will savor the texture of sweet
chocolate and crème crystallized on the
tongue of my memory
The body grows weak for the taste
Buds
Of flowers grow wildly on Susan's grave

DADDY

I was once that little girl over there with pigtails and glasses
Begging my father to run after me and play the game of chase, he never did
Well, once he did
Or twice
I remember both times

My father is not a poet

"Poetry is boring who cares about that?" He said
But I heard

"Who cares about Allison?"
The personification of all things poetic.
The winds blowing in the trees were my personal emotions. My tears were
weeping willow trees, I orated the minerals in the soil and my love for you, daddy
is bottomless

Not just Love but a reincarnated psalm

My father is not a poet

He is the hardworking man supporting 9 kids, one wife, and no "baby mamma"
Handsome, articulate, ambitious, generous, romantic, an epicure, his
paternal legacy is
Sooooo amazing

He always made sure the family had a vacation, his best was beyond GOOD ENOUGH
Daddy, I AM thankful
I mostly adore you when we talk
But we didn't talk

My father is not a poet

So we don't talk about my sophomore year in high school, we found out about
Mom's breast cancer. We don't mention her lying in bed, post chemo
...while you were at work the house was so silent
Unspoken poems sat on my mother's queasy stomach
Ghosts

There was elegy in my teenage angst
Sucking my teeth for having to come home and wash and cook and clean
Callow headed Me
As I watched her cry I became the human definition of HELPLESS

Silence
The house was pure prose

Daddy, It was like, like
Like being underwater
The walls were always gray or blue during those years

So at 15 I reached for the medicine that you've always used
And filled your shadow with my own drunkenness
So, No
We couldn't write those poems
Because
My father is not a poet

When mom died, I was the one who cleaned your vomit

There is no dirge for my inability to love a man
Unless he made me wait for him
Or ignored me

Who cares about that? Who wants to hear people write about feelings?

To heal, to heal, to heal
From head
to heel, to toe
to hell
with not writing Daddy!

We can heal this
Daddy stopped praying, because hope was buried on February 29, 1993
Hope died of breast cancer
He is now married to meantime
She folds into the wrinkles
Around his eyes
Dimming his sight

Like a slow gin fizz...

Daddy I adore every gray hair of your memory

My love for you is bottomless
I am writing the unsaid
If light represents life
Then dark represents death
Daddy see the light and
I'll write the darkness away
Because, my love for you is bottomless
Even if
You are not a poet.

VENITA

It was
PAIN
LIKE BURYING GLASS INTO EVERY INCH OF
MY SKIN
Burning & Bleeding
Like wanting to wrap my arms around a
cloud
Frustration
The day that mommy died
The day that mommy died
I understood the ECHO

Mom always wore lipstick
The color wine
Smooth and lucid
On medium full lips
Applied in the rearview
Or in the bedroom bureau mirrors

I STILL SEE HER IN THE MIRRORS

I wear wine lipstick to remember Venita
Chiseled cheek boned
Splendor
A voluptuous mother
Quiet
Gentle
"The bible is God's word Allison,
remember that"

I cannot remember that
I can only remember that you were
allowed
A cancerous thief
Raped you
Ripped your hair
Dark and wavy from it's glory
Mommy is illegitimately at rest

She is the earth's cargo

But I keep dreaming you alive, mommy
Outside of the pictures
Walking
Living
A separate life

Her departure into the unknown
Takes on a life of it's own
Because she is illegitimately
Eternally
At rest

Though she was high above mountains of
more
Venita loved New York, but
She was a southern country girl
Sewing stitches into the fabric so that
the bloodlines bind 9 siblings

She was the eldest child of three

She was more than, "was"
So much more than, "was"

The praise before the curse

How do I summarize my mother?
Never enough ink
To catalogue
Every
Treasured detail
Every heartbeat
Every drop of love
Every memory now unbearable

Garrulous Waters

I am still too small to fully embrace my mom

Every memory clouds my heart with smoke

I am just too small

She was not at my wedding
Or my divorce

No adult mothering on telephone conversations

I was still small when she passed

My mother is now the earth's cargo
And I am still

Just too small

*I CAN SMELL MY MOTHER'S TOUCH DEEP UNDERNEATH THE SKIN
ON MY RIGHT HAND*

IT IS NOT A SMALL SMELL

EVEN AFTER TEN YEARS

DEFINITIONS

ACUTE: *Extremely sharp or severe; intense*

TRAUMA: *A serious injury or shock to the body; an emotional wound or shock that creates substantial, lasting damage to the psychological development of a person, often leading to neurosis; an event or situation that causes great distress and disruption*

DENIAL: *An unconscious defense mechanism characterized by refusal to acknowledge painful realities, thoughts or feelings*

DELUSIONS: *A false belief strongly held in spite of invalidating evidence, especially as a symptom of mental illness*

MENTAL: *Of or relating to the mind; intellectual*
               Executed or performed by the mind; existing in the mind

ILLNESS: *Poor health resulting from disease of body or mind; sickness*

POWERLESS: *Lacking strength or power; helpless and totally ineffectual*

ACQUIESCENCE: *Passive assent or agreement without protest*

CINNAMON JANET - AKA- Denise My Sister Scarred

Hi Allie, How are you, this is Cinnamon. Cinnamon Janet. I am here in New York, I just got a calling card and I am going to sell jewelry and computers but I know that I am being followed...If the phone cuts off I will call you back. How are youuuu? How are the kids? I miss you Allie. Did you know that you have children here in New York; the government stole your eggs when you were a baby. I saw a picture of you in the window, you were with a man and a little baby, it was an advertisement. Was that man your husband? Well, I am going to marry Edgar; I know that he is having me followed. He and I are good friends, we are always walking together, and his new chauffeur will not let me talk to him when I go to his office. I hate his driver. I also wanted to tell you that I am going to make movies from this computer program that you can film movies...Allie, I miss you, are you drinking enough juice? You need to be sure to have carrot juice with pears and apples and to drink Nutrament everyday...It is cold out here, I sleep at the Laundromat, I can't sleep at the shelter anymore, they kept stealing stuff from my cart and someone planted a camera under my bed...They kept listening to me and following me, when I make my movie I'll be a Millionaire and I won't have to be so poor anymore. I will buy a big house for you and me and Tahjamere and your kids, I just need $1200 to buy the computer program and then I can make the movies and do the editing, but anyway this phone is running out of money. I love you Allie...(click, the phone line is dead)

How deep does the phone line go?
Into the heart of the matter?
&
What matter
Does it
matter?
Because
Schizophrenia is another perception
Of reality altered by paranoia
I miss the sister I used to know
I miss the sister that I understood
I do not miss her phone calls....

Allison A. Baker

NO ESCAPE

I am sitting watching TV
Being lazy mentally
Slack of my mind
Unkind
Can't find TV remotely
I thus crawl into my psyche
To improvise mind slumber
Blinking to laugh
Cuz watery eyes threaten
And I live through the words on the
screenplay

X marks the spot where I awaken
Bid farewell to my loaf of rest
I wake to wonder
To feed my hunger
Slow chewing on words
That find their print place
Face up in my journal
February 29th
Read
Silence
See me moved beyond
The death of millions
Beyond
"Five children dead in a fire
News at five"
Four
Three

Two
One girl who regrets never having
shed tears
While her mother's voice echoes
within her mind chambers
She burning to embrace
Mama's ghost
She knowing only her fight
To stay one step behind reality
One blink before the tears
One brick behind the build of years
She's swallowing her fears
This girl
This me
Continuing my legacy of an 80 proof
exodus
That denies my dry eyes any moisture
Soak my sorrows in bourbon's bath
Kiss my lips Mr. Heineken
Do it again
Do it again
And now I've lost the kissing game
Tossed my sense down a well
Where I wish deaf ears to mama's
ghost
But I'll always
Always
Remember her smile...

"EXCUSE ME NURSE, WHERE IS MY BABY"

I couldn't believe those words were actually mine to use...mine to choose..."my baby" When I looked at the fragile creature, sleeping in my arms strange and disjointed from the life that I've always known. My arms felt abnormal in the new crooked position around her body, trying to be as gentle as I already know to be, but still I felt so unsure. Emotions washing over me were more profound than losing my mother. I was now a mother. I kept thinking how this little body was inside of my body all that time...I was astounded, and scared. Here was the reason I stopped drinking, the person I was preparing for, reading about, my own personal celebrity. My little soul mate...me? I was at a loss for words. I was a young mother (19) and had to accustom myself to the sacrifices, getting up in the middle of the night to make bottles. My body ached all over as if I was running a marathon, as if I was being trained for some kind of Olympic event, and the fact of the matter is that I was. I am still training for this event called motherhood. Every day with each turn of the road and every twist of fate, I am being refined, enlightened, and disciplined for the biggest event taking place in the universe, motherhood. I am the echo to the last piano chord, the honor is solid in my heart...I know that I am in good company with my mother, grandmother and ancestors'...mothers to this earth; this is not a new dance.

"she's so beautiful, oh my god, how beautiful. Ican'tbeliveit, I can'tbeleiveit, ican'tbeleiveit,
"she's so beautiful, oh my god, how beautiful. Ican'tbeliveit, I can'tbeleiveit, ican'tbeleiveit,
"she's so beautiful, oh my god, how beautiful. Ican'tbeliveit, I can'tbeleiveit, ican'tbeleiveit,"
she's so beautiful, oh my god, how beautiful. Ican'tbeliveit, I can'tbeleiveit, ican'tbeleiveit,
"she's so beautiful, oh my god, how beautiful. Ican'tbeliveit, I can'tbeleiveit, ican'tbeleiveit,
"she's so beautiful, oh my god, how beautiful. Ican'tbeliveit, I can'tbeleiveit, ican'tbeleiveit,

My baby

Allison A. Baker

EARTH TO SEED

I am reborn

You are the personification of my ideology
And the deification of my kisses
You are my denial of a mortal life
Immortal I am within you, as I grow
You grow

I am reborn

You represent the paradigm of my entire yearning
The kiss of transcendence in your gentle smile is dimpled deeply into my heart
I give it all to you

Hopesyearnstearsprayer and adoration

You are my child
My denial of a mortal life
My intimate mantra

I am born again

FAMILY TREE

Sitting on the sofa...my knees on my stomach...the girls are combing their black Barbie dolls straight hair (?) when they look at me...what do they see? I start to think about which pain would be worse living with a dead mother...versus the live mother and the pain I cause them from my choices and living with me and the choices that I've made...them watching the hopelessness on my face, seeing the desperation that I suffer and my loss of faith. They can't name it now, the vulnerability that I embody, but when they do eventually learn the words, will they call my fear a lack of love for them, while they are the only reason I exist...why I finally stopped slicing my wrists...I fear that this love is not enough...and words fail me right on the tip of my tongue see, these daily struggles cause me this sadness, the pain hits my heart and freezes the words on the tip of my tongue so that when I am home and want to tell those children how much I love them...I'm stuck with three words and a cliché kiss.

They are too young to swim deep and I'm busy trying not to drown by treading water until I can get to the shallow end...maybe one day reach the shore...maybe one day I'll tell them more...I live a lifetime in the world of maybe...it's the only world I've ever known...and, I'll keep trying to show them a better one...painting with flawed hands, this picture as real as what I know real to be...I'm trying not to draw too many cages...too many monsters...too many weapons...or even too much of my own food but the art of life sketches with footsteps and tears...child, life for me ain't been no crystal stair...ain't been no masterpiece...ain't been no awards...but my reward is this umbilical lifeline...mother to child...I am reborn as a family tree...three branches growing...my reward is each of you (my children)...my babies...my silver lining for every day...my stripes...my wisdom...my walking, talking, prayer and praise...my story will never end...nor this poem...love unsaid in unspoken alchemy roots deeply into this earth...this family tree...my children and me...this story will never end...so shall it be...Amen

Allison A. Baker

DRUM THE SKINS

My stretch marks are my fears inscribed
Embedded into the definition of my MOTHER HOOD
A reality profane
Emblazoned on brown skin

MOTHERHOOD three times defined
Carved MOTHER

The memory of childbirth can no longer be a nuisance...

RAIN FALLS INTO THE OCEAN ON ANY GIVEN DAY

PUZZLE

A man

A woman

Two people

Lost in the roar

Of the city

Find themselves

Wrapped up

In the hairy arms of lust

Together

They unfold each other

Explaining away the mysteries of their mind

Hoping to find the missing pieces

Wanting to connect

In this puzzle of society

We are pieces

We are scattered

We are shifted about

Looking for a fit

Allison A. Baker

"How do I know if it's right?
It's been wrong before."

When we embrace
I feel myself collecting my soul
Searching among the pieces
And I feel the puzzle
Come together

OBSESS

Even now

I kiss him on his shoulder
While he is asleep
My lips have landed
On his skin
Bringing cease
To the gnawing within me

Bliss
Exists
As satisfaction within me

And all I am is crazy
For being in love
With the dead

You see,
Corpses lie
And cannot stand
And most times
Will not respond
Much like how
You have no requite for me
And obsess I will
Confess, as I am guilty
The sin of loving the dead
And watching this dead man
Asleep yet drowning in his dreams
So completely unaware of me
Blowing kisses
At his armpits

Why am I tormenting me?
Chasing ghosts
And your soul is
Dead regarding me
It is empty to all that I am feeling

Allison A. Baker

I am begging for a miracle
A wish for a magic spell
So that solitude
No longer be my friend
And then I close my eyes
And then there was silence

And then there was silence

ROSES

Your Lies

Were anger

Drenched in my Love

Heated missiles thrust into my heart

Painting tears

Salty on my face

Seconds weighing on my back

Pounding in my head

Roses have sprouted on the grave of truth

Brought death to my hopes
Brought death to my hope

Y yo no comprendo
I don't understand

No, my man
I don't understand
You

Bringing me the blues

With your false lips
Wrapped around my neck

Hanging me with my broken heart

And my tears fill glass bottles
In sizes of 40 ounces
And speaking of bottles
I make bottles for our child
Who sprouted from my loins
Unattended, unnoticed by you
Well noticed by your lies
Yet she has your eyes

I pray that she doesn't have my thighs
Or my eyes
And keeps her thighs closed

AMEN

HE

He

Held
A morsel
Within his palm
Tempting
My hunger
For the hospice
Of his embrace

There I
Attended often
But
All I am is folly
Because Love never won the war

Love cannot mediate
Black deception
From diamond purity
Purely
My love
Faceted
For
He once held me...
But
All I am is folly
Because love never won the war

One:
The war
Was not with me
A casualty
Casually
Naïve
Though not blameless

Nonetheless
I did not bury shame
I was true to you

Two:
You
Must understand
That I was true

With my fire

And it burned only
For He
Wore apathy
As underwear
He offered
What he could not give
What he could not live
What he could not give

I will not over-dramatize

Because all I am is folly
And love never won the war
Though I am fighting for the truth
Which was once
Elusive
Against my hunger
Now is ulcerated
As I stomach
Your betrayal
With She
Deemed forever nameless
Her countless faces

She
Smelling the skin
That I once
Lived in
And my head hangs low
As a seed grows
And

This child's love has
The River Nile depth
For
He
Whom I once loved
Him I once loved...

Allison A. Baker

ONE MORE DANCE

Standing in kitchens

In the heat

Overlooking pots

At silver gleaming memories of
Lost battles
Lost lovers

Cause my tears to fall like rain
As my soul accepts a slap

Cuz my pain is old
And I'm steady high on hope
The best dope for the blues
I am immobile as I wait for you
In your cashmere brown
Skin
Soft lips
(Need my kisses)
Bronze eyes

And your smell

Watch as I twist and twirl
Two steps forward
Four steps back

To square one

Back to you

And I am offering
This delicate flesh
I'm dressed in
My heavy heart
Pumping blood
My soul is at risk beneath your
fingers
And it's all too thick to throw away
Instead
Cast your eyes again upon me my love
Promise

Promise me
No more heat
In love's kitchen

I cannot withstand the fire

I'm not here to be burned
It's just that I came back to you
For one more dance
One more chance
In love's kitchen

NOBODY'S FOOL

You will not have the chance
To give me an excuse
I already know how the blue moon
Doesn't shine down on my blackness
Despite the surge filling my heart
With every beat
Like coconut drums play
And monkeys laugh in the distance
My love beats exotic to this universe

Of you

Yet

You think stars twinkle fairy songs
And birds sing songs that lust for generations

Yet love

Love made millions

And is something
That can't be scraped off the bottom of your shoe
Though you try

&This can place
A space of confusion in baby girl's trust

I mean maybe love lost to lust

I am not the enemy

I mean maybe love lost to lust

You're not gonna have the chance
To give me an excuse

Allison A. Baker

OF MICE AND MEN

When God created Adam and Eve, he
taught the first lesson of life
The first human guideline

It was about decisions

We give birth to decisions every day,
yet we are living in times where
decisions
Can be balled up into a garbage bag
(murdered baby?)

Decisions are hid
In a society of adultery

Fear

Guilt

Pride

A mouse tucks away his decisions
In a paper bag excuse
Or a glass pipe explanation
Or in an angry closed fist
And he scurries up into the walls
These mice
Or some say men

Are the pests that dwell in the walls of
our homes
The escape artist who never has any
plans
For staying
His whole performance is for his finale
His exit
His decisions aren't real
They don't come from that deep space in
your heart
Because somehow with the passage of
time
That space has been erased...

People used to stand by their plans
And principle came from the core

A man had plans

Decisions that he could stand by
Decisions he could live by
And even if he failed
He kept trying
Until he had gold
But the rush for gold is over
The result is at the bottom of the river
Treasure sits awaiting cultivation
Yet very few mice will swim deep

SUGAR DADDY

There are no more fathers
And it's a lonely place

When daddy
Don't want you on his knee

When daddy
Let some cat catch his tongue
He won't tell you that it's gonna be
alright

When daddy
Is somehow gone

In some way

He's gone
And you are left to search for his
replacement

Someone to watch over me
Someone that knows that I ain't made
out of stone
Or steel

My flesh is warm
And my heart pumps blood
And I got some heavy emotions
"You ain't got to always be hurting me"
Smacking my face for every smile
Smacking my face for every hope
Like we are soldiers
Destined to live tears and tears and
tears
In this war game

As a casualty

As a bastard

As a soldier

Displaced

Searching for some warmth
A place to call home
It's cold outside

& I am cold

Allison A. Baker

GUNFIRE

There was no gunfire
At Jesus
Yet
He understands
The ghetto

And how it lies
Within the heart of men

Certain men who twist love

Incomplete they hurt love

Hit love

Miss love

They will never understand

The valley of light that caused love...

They will never understand

Meanwhile
The greed that selfishness bore
Allows the rape of love
Fits like a glove is the only
Refrain

These men have hearts
Where shallow waters
Allow no distance of travel
Yet they walk the streets
Allowing themselves no future
No future with out love
Only illiberal gunshots
And selfish warriors stalking
At war in the darkness
Of their ignorance
And lord knows that
In the graveyards lies the truth
There in the dirt lay truth
Listen to me...
And I will tell you that
Falsehoods may hug your shoulders

Deceit may dry your tears
But
God is love
God is love
God is always love
But you are not knowing
You are not loving
Your souls are slowly dying
In the darkness
But
Without the light
You will never understand...

KISS

I really, really miss
Enjoying the passion and promise
And soul
Of a kiss
Flowers on my lips

And I really, really
Miss
Being embraced
By eyes that watch me
Like I am the only woman
On earth
And I am selfish
And I am foolish
Because those moments are
One among one million
Other moments
That, too pass
Too fast
But I wish
For just one kiss
In one moment
It will be endless

Allison A. Baker

TO MY ONE NIGHT MAN

I begged the universe to
Hold the morning
For a few more hours
Until I could at least believe
The possibility that
The arms holding me
Were
And that the softness in my heart
Would stay
As we lay
But
Morning is too clever
And rushed to bring my reality
Really, I am a foolish girl
Too foolish for pretty words
& Sugar promise
& Soul
Tongue
Kissing
Too foolish
Too foolish
Too soon

He is aloof
Like an altar
A man of the moon
Who
Nurtures me
He's serious in my estimation
Kind as warm rain
Gentle as cashmere
He is loved
Like the sun
Like hope peeping out from a cloud
On the days that I am gray
I am wishing for the sun
In him
Yearning for
Him
His
Infinite words
Recycled through genius

And spoken in the tempo
Of Jazz
& Calypso
This man
So patient
So passionate
So gentle

His kiss
Generates my soul
Gyrate my hips
Like on a string

"Pull my string again"

Pull my string
Until I cannot bear another touch
Until we meet again

Allison A. Baker

OCEAN PULL

I am watching the ocean
The waves of the sea
Come to me and pull away
Come to me
Like you
Come to me
To wash over me
Salty on me
Sweaty on me
You do not miss me
The way that I miss you
As I watch you
Pull away
My tears return to the sea
And then the sky
Where the air is hemmed in
With layers that I cannot see
I cannot see me
Without you

LUSHNESS

Writer artfully contrive me into your lushness
Color me into a gray scene, green in a gray landscape
Translate my soul with your musings
Writer
Erotically incite me to touch my wetness
Excite me to moans and gyrations
Writer who writes sweetness
Meet me in my fantasy
And capsize my loneliness
Interpret my fears through each passage
Writer please write into me and onto my skin
Your inscriptions of honey words
Sweet on me
With each stroke
Sweet on me

Allison A. Baker

COMPROMISE

There are flowers on the grave
Within the grave buried
My wisdom
Buried
I buried it
To lay burned and scarred
Underneath you
Burrowing deeply into me
Plunging flames into me
Though explanations the next day were cold

The next day
And the day after
Were
Cold

So goes the weather

THE FLOOD

FLOOD

What did they think

When the rain really did come???
And they asked

Was it supposed to be so hard????

The blue tiles

Extended

Throughout

And within them

Like pearls

Hardened

In response
To what was placed
As an irritation...
And it turns out that
The incubation
Spanned over thousands of years
Before the day
Finally dawned
That the rain yielded

Allison A. Baker

POETRY

I always want to share my words
My rhythm words
Not rhyme
Written line by line
In my own time
Pen in hand
It's my only push against the crushing
Power posing as ink
What do you think?
I mean haven't you noticed
That laughter falls like rain
Falls like tears
And it all sounds like pain
To me
And we all know
That misery must be shared
Among us animals
Unidentified us
Who sit in poetry readings
Fellow poets
Who share the beat
The rhythm
Of graveyards
Ghosts passing through ink
Finding cemetery in my voice
Find warning in my voice
I am a poet

GARRULOUS

Watch the circle of the moon
Pulling the ocean tides
Look...the circle of my pregnant
womb
Listen
My mama used to tell me
Simple explanations
Loud exclamations
Of defamation
Though no less love
Though no less love
But
Love is redundant
And during the time
Of the full moon
The tides are redundant
Though no less lovely
Though no less beauty
Full of hope
I have often
Bitten the wind
To spite my own heart
And learn the lessons
Of unrequited love
The lessons of barriers
For the flesh
Which have tested
My passion
has flowed with the wants
of others
I am not the only one...though
Millions of tears
Have fallen
To the grounds of divorce
Sistergirl and babygirl
Discovered

Diss
Covered
By lies
Yet his eyes were so humble
"He said that he loved me"
He said that
He said that
That which he said
Is redundant

Though no less painful
Love
And this love concerns me...
My brow wrinkles and I will sit
Like déjà vu
Just like you
On many occasions
Sat down and watched the moon
That is watching centuries
Form circles
That is redundant
Though no less infinite
Circles that stand immortal
Containing history of fleshly passion
Earthly mundane heat
Longing lessons of
Love even exists
Distorted in a fist
And in kisses
It is slashing tires
Loving a love child
Bearing a nation
In songs
Poetry
Painting
Sculpture

Allison A. Baker

Verses
Narrative
Kisses
Touches
Embrace it

Though love no less absolute
Though love is no less

Symbiotic
Though love is no less
Redundant
Love is
Moving in circles
Through time
After time
After time

SESAME STREET

Empty bowl
Cast to the shadows
Of my desk

Old man
Cast to the shadows
Of the subway stairs
Leading up
To the sidewalk and the sunlight
Where brightness
Accentuates darkness
And daylight skips the shadows
As I walk past old man beggar
Up the stairs
And away to my desk
With a growl in my stomach
Ringing in my ears
And my eyes are on bare feet
Wrapped in dirt rags
The old bum
Screaming his poverty
His growling soul
My growling stomach
Imbalance of the scales
Dark against light
Stairways going up
Empty stomachs
Empty hearts
And another sunny day

Allison A. Baker

OPIUM SONG

The sky is vibrant blue
And soft like
Soft arrogance
In a world such as this
Under this sky
I have the the audacity to feel the pain
of others
To intimately know
The trail of tears
On the human face
Under this vibrant blue sky
How can I face
The inhumanity of wickedness
And the crooked thinking of wars?
Destroying the innocent
Sacrificing lives to the ruling warriors
Ruling warriors
Of flesh
Sanctioning necessities
To ransom
For the attention of the opposed
How many must die
This time
How many
Of the women
And children
Will suffer the irony

Of contrary spirits
When will humanity see the blue?
Indigo
& I am too soft
Too sensitive to accept
The ride of death
The ride of hunger
The ride of corruption
How can I take it?
How do we?

WHY RATIONALIZE MADNESS?
WHY RATIONALIZE CRUELTY?
WHY RATIONALIZE THE DEATH OF A
HUMAN SPIRIT?

Although
Love is sleeping on the streets buried
under the billows of long gone sanity.
Sanity long gone in today's and
tomorrows

Faith is the opium of us people

Faith is the opium of those people
Faith is the opium of us
The people...

CARDBOARD HOME

Where I am home
Where I am Hooooome
Hmmmmm

Home

The home of my childhood
Was my religion
The house where I understood God
His purpose for creation, his word
&
Keeping his laws was the objective for God's Love
God's laws were my religion
My childhood home

But I left home

Then branded with a tattoo of guilt
Because I fall short of that which is holy
I am the swine devouring pearls
Transforming pearls of wisdom
Into the shit of fornication
And bullshit bastardation

The good word gives counsel

"Do not provoke your children to wrath, but nurture them in the lord"

I am full of contrition
Becuz I nurtured them in wrath
Becuz they were born in sin
From a fuck me refrain
The dope of my thighs
A deep dopamine high

"Hush baby don't you cry"

Allison A. Baker

Mama's gotta eat some humble pie
But
Humility belongs to the prophets
And I am merely really a fool
Becuz I should have stayed home

For now I live in a homeless shelter
With three children
And my fanciful tattoo
Though this guilt is an old skin
It ages my ambition for life
Makes me question
What will I teach my children?
If I can't learn the lesson?

It seems that I am becoming the lesson
An empty life alienated from God
Homeless
Yes
I said, "Homeless"
But
"I will work for food"
I've worked for Philosophical empty calories that
Cause the voices in my head to curse me with every defamation
Becuz I swim shallow in the depth of spirituality
Home now seems so elusive
A sweet song fading out from the walls of my current shelter
My old memories of home
Though I am at home with this guilt
I dwell in a shelter that
Lacks security
Rain on the cardboard box
Seeps
How wet do I have to get before I return home?
Verse (step) by verse (step)
Down the paved path
To my childhood home
Washed clean in the blood of the lamb
Washed clean

In my life I am always looking for the line between trying too hard
And not trying hard enough
Between trying too hard and not giving a fuck
Between rushing to be early and hurrying up because I am always late
Waiting for God or needing help with my faith
Believing in my own power or believing in fate
My destiny it seems is not to know what I claim to know
When daily disappointments destroy my ego blow by blow
To say that I am frustrated is an understatement but by saying nothing is to truly say what I know
So without my ego, I roll with the flow but with my ego I go toe to toe with every unseen foe

Daily disappointments destroy my ego

"LIFE WITHOUT THE ID"

FROM A PUDDLE TO A STREAM UNTIL THE OCEAN

IN THE MIRROR

In the mirror
Is my image
My hair
My eyes
My nose
My mouth
Defines me
I see me
But you don't see me

And

I won't be
I can't be
I won't be
I can't be

Your misrepresentation fulfilled
Your ghetto fool, pop a pill
Neck popping rolling shrill
Foot dragging baby bill
Crackhead, "here cop a feel"

Chill
Chill
Chill

I am made of steel
Overcoming adversity you
mutherfuckers could never know
Can't see me in no media hype
Corporate machine,
Bottom line
Dollar driven
Bullshit writer staff
Buffoon cartoon caricature
Falling short of my true beauty

No alchemy to me in TV
No radio reference of my desire
SEXUALITY
I am more regal than any Queen Bee
My attitude is not an attitude
It is
My fear of eviction, that I can lose my
job
Or can't stretch my last dollar
Are there really no good men?
"He said he would bring the money, did he
lie again?"

Doesn't he even love his children?

Where is MY daddy?

I wish my mother wasn't dead &
Why is it that even though I do the work
of three vice presidents
My salary is the same as the cleaning
crew?

I raise my chin
Again
Because I'm gonna get my degree
I'm gonna get my grant money
I'm gonna teach these children all about
Me
The
Me
My children see
Will be
The
Me
That I see

Allison A. Baker

In the mirror
And like the image in the pond, my
children will mirror
The defined parts of me in reflections
On my poetic streams of thoughts
On my poetic streams of life
Reflecting on being me
Not defined
Confined
Or lowered by
Man to man
Woman to woman
Stratification situations

I represent a whole
Of a generation
Who are self-actualized personified
Fate fighting, truth seekers

Beauty reigning
Obstacles overrun

SO don't play me like no rap song
1,2, 1,2
Fuck you, Fuck you

The truth of me will not be televised
I am the truth before your eyes
I am much more than my thigh size
I am much more than much more
God's purpose personified
Representing
Me
The
Me
That I see
The Me within me
I will affirm her
I will AFFIRM

SHE'S ON TIME

I am yet a man
Compared to the woman who is divine

POWERFUL

She put cobwebs on the soul of monkeys
To despise their evolution
And placed the earth in it's invisible cage
She is in the air
Waltzing the ancient dance of love
Invented in the rhythm of her heartbeat
This woman walks within an echo
Blowing the winds of a solstice
That deify etchings on the leaves
She leaves to make me wait
And while her away
She is lost in the lapse of sound
Yet found in the spaces of eternity
And she sits in among the ghosts and genes of generations
On the right hand of the goddess
The woman is TIME
And I am only a man
Unable to wage war with this mortality
As time bombs explode across the skin on my face
Leaving trails of defeat in my hair and on my brow
How can I challenge her?
Time is divine
She, is despised by men
Her power to daunt the human soul
One day she sat on my stomach
Loyally haunting me
As I lose the war day after day after day
Laughing into the distance of my memories
Time capsulated in poem
Though I lose the war
Day after day
Amen

ABOUT THE AUTHOR

Allison Baker was born on March 23, 1975 in Jamaica, Queens, New York. She is the youngest of nine children. She relocated to Broward County, Florida in 1996 and currently resides in Deerfield Beach. She has been writing poetry since the age of eight. After having her oldest daughter, she began to write poetry intently and began to read at poetry readings in New York, one particular venue was then called, "the Brooklyn Moon" café.

She relocated to Florida and endured unimaginable trauma in her family. This is when she began writing to survive, as she often says about this harrowing time, "the tragedy is not easy to convey...it like my heart is filled with garrulous waters...rising and full of waves." She performs and reads her work at several South Florida poetry Venues: Dada's, Mellow Dramatic, Ghetto Poetry, The Poet's Corner, and The Literary café.

Her first book entitled: Garrulous Waters: an intimate autobiographical poetic represents the culmination of her collection of poems. The compilation dates range from 1995 to 2003. The book is a creative, poignant and absorbing recount of her life experiences. Topics include: love, relationships, spirituality, self-affirmation and the remembering of lost loved ones.

"I write not out of egotism, I write to survive"

She is a true survivor, representing the healing power of poetry. Allison is currently pursuing a Bachelor's degree in psychology, as a sophomore at Florida Atlantic University. She also sits on the committee for, "The Children's Cultural Center" as a grant writer and marketing mentor. She works full time in accounting and most importantly is a mother to Chelsea, Gabrielle and Nina

www.ingramcontent.com/pod-product-compliance
Lightning Source LLC
Chambersburg PA
CBHW020357290526
45785CB00005B/2327